T0024964

STICKER ENCYCLOPEDIA

TRUCKS

DK | Penguin Random House

Project Editors Kritika Gupta, Robin Moul
US Senior Editor Shannon Beatty
Project Art Editors Kanika Kalra, Charlotte Bull
Art Editors Mohd Zishan, Bhagyashree Nayak
Assistant Art Editor Simran Lakhiani
Managing Editors Penny Smith, Monica Saigal
Managing Art Editor Ivy Sengupta
DTP Designers Ashok Kumar, Dheeraj Singh
Project Picture Researcher Sakshi Saluja
Jacket Designers Rashika Kachroo, Charlotte Bull
Production Editor Dragana Puvacic
Senior Production Controller Inderjit Bhullar
Delhi Creative Heads Glenda Fernandes, Malavika Talukder
Special Sales and Custom Publishing Executive Issy Walsh
Publisher Francesca Young
Deputy Art Director Mabel Chan
Publishing Director Sarah Larter

First American Edition, 2022
Published in the United States by DK Publishing
1450 Broadway, Suite 801, New York, New York 10018
Copyright © 2022 Dorling Kindersley Limited
DK, a Division of Penguin Random House LLC
22 23 24 25 26 10 9 8 7 6 5 4 3 2 1
001-327032-July/2022

Material previously published in Super Trucks (2013) and Monster Machines (1998).

All rights reserved.
Without limiting the rights under the copyright reserved above, no part of this publication may be reproduced, stored in or introduced into a retrieval system, or transmitted, in any form, or by any means (electronic, mechanical, photocopying, recording, or otherwise), without the prior written permission of the copyright owner.
Published in Great Britain by Dorling Kindersley Limited.
A catalog record for this book is available from the Library of Congress.
ISBN: 978-0-7440-5668-6

DK books are available at special discounts when purchased in bulk for sales promotions, premiums, fund-raising, or educational use. For details, contact: DK Publishing Special Markets, 1450 Broadway, Suite 801, New York, New York 10018
SpecialSales@dk.com

Printed and bound in China

For the curious
www.dk.com

MIX Paper | Supporting responsible forestry FSC™ C018179 FSC www.fsc.org

This book was made with Forest Stewardship Council™ certified paper – one small step in DK's commitment to a sustainable future. For more information go to www.dk.com/our-green-pledge

About this book

HOW TO USE THIS BOOK

Read the information pages and then search for the relevant stickers at the back of the book to fill in the gaps. Use the sticker outlines and labels to help you.

There are lots of extra stickers that you can use to decorate the scenes at the back of the book. It's up to you where you put them all. The most important thing is to have lots of sticker fun!

The publisher would like to thank the following for their kind permission to reproduce their photographs:
(Key: a-above; b-below/bottom; c-center; f-far; l-left; r-right; t-top)

1 Dorling Kindersley: James River Equipment (cr). **Dreamstime.com:** Igor Lovrinovic (cl). **Shutterstock.com:** Christopher Halloran (bc). **2 Dreamstime.com:** Jianghongyan (bc); Jennifer Thompson (cla); Ovydyborets (cla/stones); Zmkstudio (bl). **Shutterstock.com:** Maxim Ibragimov (br). **3 Dreamstime.com:** Jianghongyan (bl); Yaroslav Zhak (tr); Lucian Milasan (cl); Susanne Neal (cr); Photomall (br); Krischam (br/Road). **Getty Images / iStock:** CDH_Design (tc). **4-33 Dreamstime.com:** Hanna Lipchynska (Pattern). **4 Dreamstime.com:** Splav (b). **6-7 Dreamstime.com:** Jenhuang99 (Background); Steve Woods / Woodsy007 (b). **6 Dreamstime.com:** Ljupco (bc); Ovydyborets (clb). **7 Dreamstime.com:** Mbolina (cl); Ovydyborets (bc, cr); Jennifer Thompson (tr). **8 Dreamstime.com:** Photomall (b). **Shutterstock.com:** Maxim Ibragimov (bl). **8-9 Dreamstime.com:** Jgaunion (Background); Jianghongyan (bc). **9 Alamy Stock Photo:** Sheryl Watson (bc). **Dreamstime.com:** Maksim Safaniuk (tr); Ryzhov Sergey (c). **Getty Images / iStock:** Recebin (cla). **Shutterstock.com:** Maxim Ibragimov (br). **10-11 Dreamstime.com:** Ciezkitemat. **10 Dreamstime.com:** Campspot (tr); Eduard Zayonchkovski (bl). **Getty Images / iStock:** CDH_Design (cla, fbl). **Shutterstock.com:** M.Pakats (br). **11 Dreamstime.com:** Dan Van Den Broeke (cla); Yaroslav Zhak (tr); Maria Ivanova (b). **Getty Images / iStock:** CDH_Design (tc). **12-13 Dreamstime.com:** Ecophoto (Background); Keantian (b); Igormakarov (bc). **12 Shutterstock.com:** Vitalikaladdin (cra). **13 Dreamstime.com:** Antonio Gravante (br). **14-15 Dreamstime.com:** Hannelas Nicolas (Background). **14 Dreamstime.com:** Vicyphoto (tr); Wimammoth (clb). **15 Dreamstime.com:** Chernetskaya (ca, tr); Brian Rome (cra); Mbolina (bl). **Shutterstock.com:** Taylanozgurefe (b). **16 Alamy Stock Photo:** Furlong Photography (cl); Stocktrek Images, Inc. (cra). **16-17 Getty Images / iStock:** HKPNC (Background). **17 Dreamstime.com:** Ivan Cholakov (clb); Michael Turner (cra). **Getty Images:** Gallo Images (cr). **Shutterstock.com:** Neale Cousland (tl). **18 Dreamstime.com:** Dumitrina Andrusca; Andrei Shupilo (bl, b). **18-19 Dreamstime.com:** Stockr (Background). **19 Dreamstime.com:** Lucian Milasan (cr); Dmitriy Sladkov (clb); View7 (b). **20-21 Dreamstime.com:** Minyun Zhou (Background). **20 Dreamstime.com:** Roman Milert (br); Zmkstudio (cl); Maksym Yemelyanov (tr). **21 Alamy Stock Photo:** Performance Image (tr). **Dreamstime.com:** Bounder32h (b); Gestur Gslason (cl). **22 Dreamstime.com:** Larry Jordan (b); Zkruger (tr). **22-23 Dreamstime.com:** Noam Armonn (Background). **23 Alamy Stock Photo:** AA World Travel Library (b). **Dreamstime.com:** Marek Uliasz (br); Vitpho (cl). **Getty Images / iStock:** alacatr (cra). **24 Alamy Stock Photo:** Cavan Images (b). **Dreamstime.com:** Farmer (tr). **24-25 123RF.com:** Artem Konovalov. **Dreamstime.com:** Andreykuzmin (Burnt paper). **25 Alamy Stock Photo:** UrbanImages (clb). **26 Alamy Stock Photo:** Bob Barnes (cl). **Dreamstime.com:** Stefan Gottschild (bl); Michaelfitzsimmons (crb). **26-27 Dreamstime.com:** Maomaotou (Background); Danny Raustadt (bc). **27 Alamy Stock Photo:** @AJBC_1 (cl). **Dreamstime.com:** Evgeniyqw (br); Stefan Gottschild (fbr, bl). **Getty Images:** Galen Rowell (cr). **28 Dreamstime.com:** Siarhei Nosyreu (tl); Typhoonski (clb); Marek Uliasz (bl); Rangizzz (cra). **28-29 Alamy Stock Photo:** Felipe Sanchez (b). **Dreamstime.com:** Yanik Chauvin. **29 Dreamstime.com:** Wai Chung (cb, br); Siarhei Nosyreu (cr); Picstudio (cla); Maksym Dragunov (fcla). **30 Alamy Stock Photo:** Matt Gdowski / Southcreek / ZUMAPRES (cr). **Shutterstock.com:** Christopher Halloran (clb). **30-31 Dreamstime.com:** Mohammad Barahouei (Background); Pattadis Walarput. **31 Alamy Stock Photo:** J. Gleiter / Classicstock (cla); Gary Whitton (cra); PCN Black / PCN Photography (clb). **Dreamstime.com:** Andrei Bortnikau (crb). **32-33 Alamy Stock Photo:** Mark Scheuern (bc). BMW Group UK: (tc). **Dreamstime.com:** Blackboard373 (background). **34-35 Dreamstime.com:** Jareso. **36-37 Dreamstime.com:** Leonid Andronov. **38-39 Dreamstime.com:** Cateyeperspective. **40 Alamy Stock Photo:** Michele Oenbrink. **42 Dorling Kindersley:** James River Equipment (bl). **Dreamstime.com:** Artzzz (fbr); Wimammoth (tc); Ovydyborets (ca, clb/Stones, fcrb/Granite stones); Mikita Kavaliou (cra, br); Nikolayn (ca/Traffic cones, cl); Konstantinos Moraitis (c); Parkinsonsniper (c/Log, fcrb); Santos06 (clb); Dmitry Kalinovsky / Kadmy (crb); Chernetskaya (fcr); Pancaketom (bc); Steve Woods / Woodsy007 (bc/Construction Scoop); Chuyu (br/Tyre). **Shutterstock.com:** Maxim Ibragimov (cb). **43 Alamy Stock Photo:** Sheryl Watson (c). **Dreamstime.com:** Chernetskaya (tl, c/bales, fbr); Vladimir Fomin (tl/Wheel excavator); Susanne Neal (tc); Mikita Kavaliou (tc/Steering wheel, c/Steering wheel); Wimammoth (ca, cb); Deaconbrown (tr); Mbolina (cra); Pancaketom (ca/rock, ca/rock 1, cb/rock); Ovydyborets (ca/Granite stones, cl, cr/Granite stones, cb/Granite stones); Ryzhov Sergey (cl/Bulldozer); Emicristea (c/Excavator); Wisconsinart (cr); Santos06 (cb/Wheel); Aleksandr Nikolaev (cb/rocks, minerals); Jennifer Thompson (bl); Jianghongyan (bc); Photobac (br). **Getty Images / iStock:** Recebin (cra/Loading waste paper). **Shutterstock.com:** Maxim Ibragimov (cla, crb). **46 Alamy Stock Photo:** Duncan Selby (tl/Agriculture fire truck); Taina Sohlman (cra). **Dreamstime.com:** Artzzz (br); Enruta (tl); Deaconbrown (tc); Pancaketom (tc/rock); Yaroslav Zhak (tr); Nikolayn (tc/cones); Ovydyborets (cla, ca/stones); Campspot (fcl); Santos06 (fcra); Mikita Kavaliou (ca/Steering wheel); Eduard Zayonchkovski (cl, ca/excavator 1); Wimammoth (c); Wisconsinart (fcla, cr); Vladimir Fomin (clb); Dan Van Den Broeke (crb); Juri Bizgajmer (bl); Chernetskaya (fbl); Photobac (bc). **Shutterstock.com:** Maxim Ibragimov (cl/soil); M.Pakats (ca/excavator). **47 123RF.com:** Stepan Popov (cb/wrecker). **Dreamstime.com:** Svetlana Buzmakova (tr); Vladimir Fomin (ftl); Santos06 (tc); Nikolayn (tc/cones, cb/cones); Mikita Kavaliou (tc/Steering wheel, c/Steering wheel); Deaconbrown (ca); Vicyphoto (cla); Mbolina (fcla); Dmitry Kalinovsky (c); Wimammoth (fcr); Chernetskaya (fcr/bales); Brian Rome (fcr/Hay bales); Pancaketom (ftl/rock, cb); Igormakarov (clb); Liouthe (bl); Konstantinos Moraitis (crb); Wisconsinart (crb/Barrel); Stefan11 (br). **Shutterstock.com:** Maxim Ibragimov (cra/soil); Vitalikaladdin (cra). **50 123RF.com:** Stepan Popov (ftl). **Alamy Stock Photo:** Furlong Photography (ca/peterbilt); Duncan Selby (fcl/Agriculture fire truck); Stocktrek Images, Inc. (cl). **Dreamstime.com:** Artzzz (ca); Santos06 (tl, cb/Wheel); Mikita Kavaliou (tc, cla/Steering wheel, fcra); Ovydyborets (tc/Granite stones, cla); Michael Turner (tr); Konstantinos Moraitis (fcla); Wimammoth (ca/Red bricks, cr/Red bricks, crb/Red bricks, cb/Red bricks); Nikolayn (cla/cones, clb); Chernetskaya (ca/bales, fcrb); Chuyu (cra/Tyre); Jianghongyan (fcl); Ivan Cholakov (crb); Wisconsinart (fclb); Vladimir Fomin (cb); Igormakarov (cb/dump truck); Petrarichli (bl); Phadventure (br). **Shutterstock.com:** Neale Cousland (tl/Road Train); Maxim Ibragimov (cra, c, crb/soil). **51 Alamy Stock Photo:** David Chedgy (fclb); Evox Productions / Drive Images (clb); Performance Image (crb); Mark Scheuern (bc). **Dreamstime.com:** Artzzz (fcrb); Nikolayn (tc, c/cones, crb/cones); Igor Lovrinovic (tl); Criminalatt (tr); Jianghongyan (fcla); Mikita Kavaliou (ca, cla); Susanne Neal (cl); Wimammoth (ca/bricks, br); Wisconsinart (ca/Barrel, bl, fbr); Ovydyborets (ca/stones, cl/stones, cb); Santos06 (ca/Wheel, crb/Wheel); Chernetskaya (c); Lucian Milasan (cr); Konstantinos Moraitis (fcl); Chuyu (c/Tyre). **Shutterstock.com:** Maxim Ibragimov (ca/soil, clb/soil). **54 Alamy Stock Photo:** AA World Travel Library (tr); David Chedgy (c/Volkswagen Samba Bus); Evox Productions / Drive Images (clb); Cavan Images (bc). **Dreamstime.com:** Artzzz (fclb); Chernetskaya (tc); Nikolayn (tc/cones, cra, fclb/cones); Konstantinos Moraitis (tl); Pancaketom (ca); Zkruger (cla); Vitpho (cr); Mikita Kavaliou (c); Ilfede (cl); Igor Lovrinovic (fcr); Ryzhov Sergey (clb/Bulldozer); Juri Bizgajmer (cb/Dump truck); Chuyu (crb); Promicrostockraw (br). **Getty Images / iStock:** alacatr (bl). **55 123RF.com:** Stepan Popov (fclb). **Alamy Stock Photo:** @AJBC_1 (cl); Images-USA (tl); Bob Barnes (tr); Duncan Selby (cra). **Dreamstime.com:** Criminalatt (cb/Steamroller); Michaelfitzsimmons (cla); Pancaketom (ca); Mikita Kavaliou (ftr, cr, cb); Wisconsinart (fcr); Konstantinos Moraitis (cl/ambulance); Ovydyborets (fcrb); Santos06 (crb); Igormakarov (cb/dump truck); Susanne Neal (bc). **Getty Images:** General Dynamics (cr/Army Stryker vehicle); Galen Rowell (bl). **Courtesy of the National Science Foundation:** Laura Gerwin, NSF (br). **Shutterstock.com:** Maxim Ibragimov (tc, c). **58 Alamy Stock Photo:** Andrew Balcombe (crb); David Chedgy (tl); Duncan Selby (fcra); Felipe Sanchez (cla/Jeep); pbpgalleries (cr); Chris Cooper-Smith (clb); Gary Whitton (bl); PCN Black / PCN Photography (br). **Dreamstime.com:** Juri Bizgajmer (ca/Dump truck); Deaconbrown (tc); Mikita Kavaliou (tc/Steering wheel, cb); Ovydyborets (ca); Chuyu (ca/Tyre, fcl, cb/Tyre); Santos06 (ca/Wheel, fbl); Nikolayn (fcla, cra, fclb); Wisconsinart (fcl/Barrel); Ryzhov Sergey (cl); Picstudio (c); Pattadis Walarput (c/dust particles); Chernetskaya (fcl/bales, cb/bales); Konstantinos Moraitis (bc). Marchi Mobile GmbH: (tr). **59 Alamy Stock Photo:** J. Gleiter / Classicstock (tr); Duncan Selby (ca/Agriculture fire truck). **BMW Group UK:** (fcla). **Dreamstime.com:** Juri Bizgajmer (fbr); Mikita Kavaliou (tc); Chuyu (cla); Dmitry Kalinovsky / Kadmy (ca); Konstantinos Moraitis (ca/pick-up van); Chernetskaya (ca/bales, fcrb); Nikolayn (ca/cones, fclb/cones, bc/cones); Ovydyborets (ca/Granite stones, cb); Igormakarov (c); Santos06 (c/Wheel, clb); Susanne Neal (fcr); Aleksandr Nikolaev (fclb); Wisconsinart (cb/Barrel); Jennifer Thompson (cb/Compactor). **Courtesy of Mitsubishi Motors Corporation:** (bl). **Shutterstock.com:** Christopher Halloran (tl). **Toyota (GB) PLC:** (cra, fcl). **Volvo Truck Corporation:** (cr). **Waev Inc.:** (br). **62 Alamy Stock Photo:** Andrew Balcombe (cr/trailer); David Chedgy (cl); pbpgalleries (cr); Evox Productions / Drive Images (bl). **Dreamstime.com:** Artzzz (fclb); Wimammoth (tl, fcla/Red bricks, fclb/Red bricks, fcrb/Red bricks); Mikita Kavaliou (tc); Chuyu (ca, crb/Tyre); Chernetskaya (fcra, fcrb/bales); Nikolayn (cra, c, fcr, bc/cones); Santos06 (cl/Wheel, bc); Wisconsinart (ftl, clb, crb); Ilfede (cb); Jianghongyan (fcl, clb/rocks); Ovydyborets (ftr, fcla, cb/Granite stones); Konstantinos Moraitis (br). **Shutterstock.com:** Maxim Ibragimov (tr, cla, ca/soil, fcrb). **63 Dreamstime.com:** Artzzz (cra, ca/Dump truck, fbr, fcrb/Dump truck); Ovydyborets (tc); Phadventure (ftr, fcla/Concrete mixer truck, fcrb/Concrete mixer truck); Wimammoth (ftl, tr, ca/Red bricks, fcr/Red bricks, cb/Red bricks); Wisconsinart (tc/Barrel, fcr); Steve Woods / Woodsy007 (ca); Chuyu (cla/Tyre); Santos06 (ca/Wheel, cb/Wheel, bc/Wheel); Splav (cra/Crane); Igor Lovrinovic (cl); Nikolayn (c, fclb); Mikita Kavaliou (cb, fcrb, cb/Steering wheel); Photobac (cb/bulldozer); Dmitry Kalinovsky / Kadmy (clb, bc); Jianghongyan (fcra, fcla, cb/rocks, cb/rocks 1); Juri Bizgajmer (bl); Chernetskaya (fclb/bales, bc/bales); Jennifer Thompson (br). **Shutterstock.com:** Maxim Ibragimov (cla/soil, cr, crb, bc/soil). **67 123RF.com:** Stepan Popov (b/1:6). **Alamy Stock Photo:** Ahry (crb); Wacky Racing / picturesbyrob (cla); Greg Gard (ca); pbpgalleries (ca/Austin Mini); Evox Productions / Drive Images (ca/Ford F-150 STX, b/1:8); Panther Media GmbH (cl/yellow monster truck); David Chedgy (b/3:5); Duncan Selby (b/3:8). **Dreamstime.com:** Artzzz (cb, b/1:2); Criminalatt (tc, b/1:1); Wisconsinart (tc/Barrel, fcra, fcl); Charlottep68 (tr); Chuyu (ca/Tyre, b/3:2); Kerry Hill (cra); Wimammoth (cl/Red bricks, b/2:1); Mikita Kavaliou (c, b/2:8); Nikolayn (c/cones, cb/cones, b/2:3); Santos06 (c/Wheel, b/1:5); Juri Bizgajmer (c/Dump truck, b/1:9); Ovydyborets (cb/Granite stones, b/2:6); Pancaketom (b/1:3); Photobac (b/1:4); Susanne Neal (b/2:4); Dmitry Kalinovsky / Kadmy (b/2:5); Konstantinos Moraitis (ftl, b/2:7); Jennifer Thompson (b/2:9); Phadventure (b/3:1); Ryzhov Sergey (b/3:4); Igormakarov (b/3:6); Chernetskaya (b/3:7); Dmitry Kalinovsky (b/3:9). **Shutterstock.com:** Maxim Ibragimov (cl, fclb, b/3:3). **70 123RF.com:** Stepan Popov (4:6, 8:6, 12:6). **Alamy Stock Photo:** Andrew Balcombe (3:9, 7:9, 11:9); David Chedgy (2:5, 6:5, 10:5); Duncan Selby (2:8, 6:8, 10:8); pbpgalleries (3:3, 7:3, 11:3); Evox Productions / Drive Images (4:8, 8:8, 12:8). **Dreamstime.com:** Artzzz (4:2, 8:2, 12:2); Wimammoth (1:1, 5:1, 9:1, 13:1); Nikolayn (1:3, 5:3, 9:3, 13:3); Susanne Neal (1:4, 5:4, 9:4, 13:4); Dmitry Kalinovsky / Kadmy (1:5, 5:5, 9:5, 13:5); Ovydyborets (1:6, 5:6, 9:6, 13:6); Konstantinos Moraitis (1:7, 3:6, 5:7, 7:6, 9:7, 11:6, 13:7); Mikita Kavaliou (1:8, 5:8, 9:8, 13:8); Jennifer Thompson (1:9, 5:9, 9:9, 13:9); Phadventure (2:1, 6:1, 10:1); Chuyu (2:2, 6:2, 10:2); Ryzhov Sergey (2:4, 6:4, 10:4); Igormakarov (2:6, 6:6, 10:6); Chernetskaya (2:7, 6:7, 10:7); Dmitry Kalinovsky (2:9, 6:9, 10:9); Aleksandr Nikolaev (3:1, 7:1, 11:1); Wisconsinart (3:2, 7:2, 11:2); Deaconbrown (3:4, 7:4, 11:4); Jianghongyan (3:5, 7:5, 11:5); Vladimir Fomin (3:7, 7:7, 11:7); Igor Lovrinovic (3:8, 7:8, 11:8); Criminalatt (4:1, 8:1, 12:1); Pancaketom (4:3, 8:3, 12:3); Photobac (4:4, 8:4, 12:4); Santos06 (4:5, 8:5, 12:5); Juri Bizgajmer (4:9, 8:9, 12:9). **Shutterstock.com:** Maxim Ibragimov (2:3, 6:3, 10:3). **71 123RF.com:** Stepan Popov (2:6, 6:6, 10:6). **Alamy Stock Photo:** Andrew Balcombe (1:9, 5:9, 9:9, 13:9); pbpgalleries (1:3, 5:3, 9:3, 13:3); Evox Productions / Drive Images (2:8, 6:8, 10:8); David Chedgy (4:5, 8:5, 12:5); Duncan Selby (4:8, 8:8, 12:8). **Dreamstime.com:** Artzzz (2:2, 6:2, 10:2); Aleksandr Nikolaev (1:1, 5:1, 9:1, 13:1); Wisconsinart (1:2, 5:2, 9:2, 13:2); Deaconbrown (1:4, 5:4, 9:4, 13:4); Jianghongyan (1:5, 5:5, 9:5, 13:5); Konstantinos Moraitis (1:6, 3:7, 5:6, 7:7, 9:6, 11:7, 13:6); Vladimir Fomin (1:7, 5:7, 9:7, 13:7); Igor Lovrinovic (1:8, 5:8, 9:8, 13:8); Criminalatt (2:1, 6:1, 10:1); Pancaketom (2:3, 6:3, 10:3); Photobac (2:4, 6:4, 10:4); Santos06 (2:5, 6:5, 10:5); Juri Bizgajmer (2:9, 6:9, 10:9); Wimammoth (3:1, 7:1, 11:1); Nikolayn (3:3, 7:3, 11:3); Susanne Neal (3:4, 7:4, 11:4); Dmitry Kalinovsky / Kadmy (3:5, 7:5, 11:5); Ovydyborets (3:6, 7:6, 11:6); Mikita Kavaliou (3:8, 7:8, 11:8); Jennifer Thompson (3:9, 7:9, 11:9); Phadventure (4:1, 8:1, 12:1); Chuyu (4:2, 8:2, 12:2); Ryzhov Sergey (4:4, 8:4, 12:4); Igormakarov (4:6, 8:6, 12:6); Chernetskaya (4:7, 8:7, 12:7); Dmitry Kalinovsky (4:9, 8:9, 12:9). **Shutterstock.com:** Maxim Ibragimov (4:3, 8:3, 12:3)

Cover images: *Front:* **Alamy Stock Photo:** Greg Gard c; **Dreamstime.com:** Oleksandr Bondarenko b, Konstantinos Moraitis cl, Vitpho cr; **Getty Images / iStock:** artorn; *Back:* **Dreamstime.com:** Artzzz cr, Ivan Cholakov cb, Enruta cl, Liouthe cra, Igor Lovrinovic tc; **Getty Images / iStock:** artorn; *Spine:* **Dreamstime.com:** Lucian Milasan t

All other images © Dorling Kindersley
For further information see: www.dkimages.com

Contents

Types of trucks

Trucks come in all shapes and sizes, from small pickups and mini trucks to giant ultra-class haulers that work on construction sites. Here are a few familiar trucks you may see at work around town.

FORKLIFT TRUCK

A forklift truck is a vehicle that has blades—called forks—to raise, lower, and carry goods in a warehouse, factory, or port.

GIANT CRANE TRUCK

A giant crane truck is equipped with a large crane boom that can reach high, or lift up heavy loads.

AMBULANCE

An ambulance is a lifesaving vehicle. It brings medical aid to emergencies and takes patients to the hospital.

GARBAGE TRUCK

This medium-sized truck carries trash from homes, offices, and stores to a dump or recycling center.

PICKUP TRUCK

A pickup is a light truck with an open cargo bed used for dozens of different tasks, on and off the road.

TANKER

A tanker can carry large quantities of liquids. These liquids can be chemicals, paints, gasoline, or food, such as milk or liquid chocolate.

Diggers

Diggers can do lots of different jobs with extra tools called attachments. Digging up soil and dumping mounds of rubble are just some of the jobs that these machines can do.

Bulldozer with giant blade

The blade at the front of the bulldozer has a sharp edge, which can even cut through tree trunks!

Excavator with bucket

The metal tracks of this excavator make it easier for the truck to move around at construction sites. The bucket is used to gather and load debris.

Track excavator

A track excavator usually works on construction sites, digging trenches. Instead of wheels, the excavator has metal tracks and slides along the ground.

Backhoe loader

In the backhoe loader, the driver's seat can swivel to face the front or back of the cab, as required.

Excavator with grab

Once a building has been demolished, an excavator scoops up all the dirt, concrete, and rubble left behind. The grab has big teeth, which make it ideal for the job.

FACT!

The first digger was invented over 200 years ago. Back then, it was called a steam shovel.

Wheel excavator

The driver controls the action of the excavator's arm and bucket by operating a range of levers in the cab.

Bulldozers

Bulldozers carry out some of the dirtiest work of all. They have continuous tracks or large tires, and a heavy blade that clears the ground by pushing aside rubble.

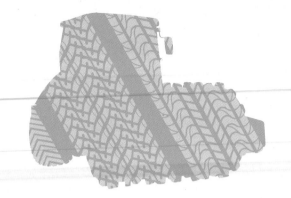

Compactor

A compactor has heavy drums with fearsome spikes that squash down hard earth to make a firm bed for a new road.

Bulldozer

Bulldozers come in different sizes. This machine can be used to repair narrow, winding roads. It's powerful enough to push away heavy debris.

Giant wheel loader

The giant wheel loader is almost ten times bigger than other wheel loaders. It digs out massive chunks of rock in a quarry.

DID YOU KNOW?
A giant wheel loader can carry a weight equal to about three elephants!

Loader

This loader can fit into smaller spaces than other machines. It can perform all kinds of jobs, such as moving bags of cement around or lifting and loading wastepaper for recycling at a warehouse.

Mining shovel

Bulldozers often work alongside machines like this giant mining shovel. They can clear away the rubble that gets dug up.

Bulldozer with ripper

This giant ripper at the back of a bulldozer lives up to its name by tearing up old tarmac and concrete as the bulldozer drives along.

Bulldozer with log shifter

This bulldozer is specially designed for forestry and lumber work. Sometimes it is fitted with a special log grapple, which can stack logs into a neat pile.

Grapplers

Grapplers have a long arm called a boom. At the end is a jaw, or claw, that can hold and lift objects. They are mostly used for picking up logs, debris, and scrap.

Truck with grappler

Excavators can be fitted with heads or buckets of different shapes and sizes, each one designed for a particular job. The driver controls them by using levers in the cab.

Truck with bucket

Some excavators are fitted with bucket attachments for clearing rubble at a construction site. The platform above its crawler tracks can swivel from side to side.

Hydraulic arm

Hydraulic arms are often fitted to trucks that need grapple attachments. To move this arm, liquid is pumped through a metal tube as it moves back and forth.

Truck with dredger

This truck has a dredging bucket that can be used to remove material from a riverbed, as water pours out from between its teeth.

Truck with a lifting magnet

A lifting magnet can lift a greater volume of material than an ordinary grapple, and it's more economical to operate.

Grapple claws

The claws on a grapple attachment are used to grab and lift scrap or pieces of metal to clear a building site.

Truck with scrap grapple

Trucks can be equipped with a special attachment for handling scrap. With its powerful clamp arm it can prepare, dismantle, and sort through piles of scrap quickly and efficiently.

FACT!

Some scrap grapplers can rapidly pull old cars apart and sort through the metal so it can be recycled.

Dumpers

Dump trucks move loose loads, such as sand, rock, coal, snow, and ice from one place to another. They are also known as tippers because their bodies can tilt upward to tip out their load when they reach their destination.

Small dumper

Although this dump truck is relatively small, it can still move loads of bricks that are twice its own weight. The bucket tilts up to dump the load.

Dump truck

Dump trucks can carry enormous loads of earth or rock to be used for construction work or in quarries and mines.

Giant dump truck

Giant dump trucks are so big that the driver needs a ladder to reach the cab. They can tilt from side to side when traveling over bumpy ground.

Tilting dump truck

With the flick of a switch the driver makes the back of the dump truck tilt upward, sending its load cascading onto the ground.

Rigid dump truck

This dump truck is rigid. It can't bend to turn tight corners, but on a big site that is not necessary.

Tipper truck

Pistons (sliding arms) lift this dumper's body high into the air so that it can "tip" out its heavy load.

Refuse truck

These trucks have machinery in the back that crunches up bags of garbage when the trash collector throws them in there.

Lifters

Many trucks are able to lift up loads and carry them from place to place. Lifter trucks come with specialized parts, like prongs, buckets, and blades.

Telescopic boom cage
The adjustable arm of this machine is called a telescopic boom. A person can stand in the cage at the top and be raised to reach high places.

Heavy tow truck
When a large vehicle like a bus breaks down, a powerful tow truck takes it away to be repaired. The lights on the top of the truck flash while it is towing.

Truck loader crane
A truck loader crane operates its extending arm to lift large steel girders. These cranes are useful for multistory building projects.

Forklift truck
Forklift trucks slide their prongs into heavy stacks of bricks. The bricks are then lifted up and transported to where they are needed.

Skid steer

The small and agile skid steer can be fitted with a range of different attachments, including a bucket, fork, blade, or broom.

FACT!

One of the biggest excavators in the world, Caterpillar 6090 FS Excavato, weighs around 1,102 tons (1,000 metric tons).

Telescopic handler

Telescopic handlers use their prongs to lift hay bales on farms. This one can lift 64 bales at a time—that's a big load!

Mass excavator

The huge mass excavator scoops up earth or rocks in a bucket attached to its long arm. It then empties the load into a dump truck to be carried away.

Extreme machines

Some trucks take it to the limit. They are the biggest, baddest haulers around, capable of carrying a giant spacecraft or hundreds of tons of rock in a single journey.

BIG RIG

Big rigs are equipped with extremely powerful engines, which can haul massive, fully loaded trailers, or pairs of trailers.

SHUTTLE CRAWLER

The shuttle crawler was used to transport a space shuttle weighing 2,205 tons (2,000 metric tons), from its assembly building to the launch pad, for liftoff.

FACT!

The shuttle crawler ran on huge steel tracks. Each of the eight tracks weighed about as much as eight elephants.

ROAD TRAIN

Used in Australia, South America, and some other parts of the world, these massive tractor units tow hefty trailers over long distances.

ULTRA-CLASS HAULER

Ultra-class haulers are true monster machines. They are able to carry more than 300 tons (272 metric tons).

JET-POWERED TRUCK

Most trucks are powered by internal combustion engines, but jet trucks harness the awesome power of jet engines—normally found in military fighter planes.

GIANT DUMP TRUCK

This truck is hauling the hopper of a giant dump truck. The road has been cleared for the truck to haul its load, which weighs more than 88 tons (80 metric tons).

Mixers

Many heavy machines are put to work at construction sites. Mixers also have an important job here.

Mounted mixer

Concrete is usually mixed in a machine, like this one mounted on a truck, to ensure batches of the same strength.

DID YOU KNOW?

Using a boom allows concrete to be pumped in a short time, and with accuracy.

Concrete mixer

The concrete mixer has a large drum that turns around. When the concrete is evenly mixed, it is ready for spreading smoothly before it sets hard.

Boom mixer

This truck pumps concrete up a long tube, called a boom, to deliver it to the top of a building.

Smoothers

After new surfaces are laid, pavers and rollers finish off the roads, making them smooth and flat.

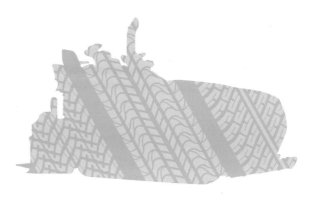

Track paver
A track paver has a noisy and smelly job to do. It lays down a mixture of warm tar and crushed rocks over the flattened earth.

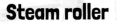

Steam roller
A steam roller usually follows after a paver. Its drums (wheels) press down on the new road surface to make it smooth and flat.

Drum roller
The roller has huge wheels called drums. It rolls over newly laid tarmac leaving behind a flat, hard surface. A steel drum weighs about 15 tons (14 metric tons).

Grader
The grader's metal blades scrape uneven surface off the ground, making it level for a new road.

Pickup trucks

Pickups are real workhorses, and are built tough and sturdy to withstand heavy use. These trucks hold the driver and passengers in the front cab, and behind that, an open bed can carry lots of different loads.

FACT!

HSV's Z-series Maloo R8 is the world's fastest production pickup truck, with a top speed of 169 mph (272 km/h).

Ford pickup truck

The Ford motor company was one of the first to build pickup trucks. The F-150 STX has a V8 engine, side airbags, and Supercab seats for up to five people.

Powerful pickup truck

The Dodge RAM D3500 Laramie is styled after big rigs. The strong steel bed behind the cab can hold loads weighing more than 5,000 lb (2,268 kg).

Chevrolet restored

Some old trucks, like this 1950s Chevrolet 3100 pickup, can be restored back to new condition.

Pickup ranger

The Ford F-250 ranger XLT has rectangular headlights, front disk brakes, and large side mirrors.

Modified pickup trucks

Pickup trucks can be modified and used for different purposes. This truck has been fitted with an equipment container.

Monster pickup truck

All monster trucks are different since their bodies are taken from different trucks.

Special delivery

Trucks are used to deliver many different things, starting from small packages, to cars, heavy furniture, and even whole buildings.

Mini hauler

Some trucks are built small and narrow so they can scoot through tight spaces in crowded cities to deliver small but important cargoes.

Container truck

Container trucks haul standard-sized steel boxes, called containers, from docks or railroad depots to their final destination.

House mover

A whole home can be raised and placed on the back of a giant flatbed trailer and towed by a truck with serious pulling power.

Articulated truck

Articulated trucks have a special joint that enables these long trucks to turn around corners smoothly.

Transporters

New cars and vans have to be delivered to showrooms and dealers. They are usually carried secured firmly on the decks of transporter trucks.

Long-haul truck

These trucks are driven by long-distance truckers going across countries or continents. Some have an extended cab with a bed and cooking facilities.

Big rig

The heaviest tractor unit (the part that pulls the trailer) used in an articulated truck is known as a big rig.

FACT!

Some big trucks are weighed on giant scales, known as truck scales, to ensure they aren't carrying loads that are too heavy.

10%

Rescue vehicles

Taking people to the hospital, putting out fires, and towing away damaged cars are some of the services trucks provide. They can be fitted with special attachments to provide on-the-spot help when people need it.

FACT!

The future of firefighting may involve robotic trucks tackling a blaze, controlled by humans a safe distance away.

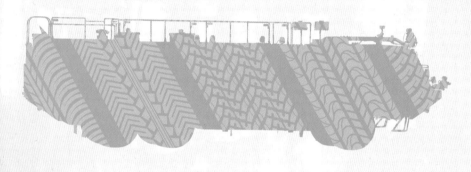

Aircraft rescue

These vehicles are built with sharp acceleration to reach a damaged aircraft quickly. They also have powerful pumps—some can spray more than 2,378 gallons (9,000 liters) of water per minute!

Fire truck

Some fire trucks can be loaded with saws, hammers, and axes so they can support other fire engines.

F.D.N.Y.
9
www.nyc.gov/fdny
F.D. N.Y.
9

Forest fire truck

A forest fire truck sprays a chemical known as a fire retardant. It helps stop bushes and trees from catching fire, and prevents forest fires from spreading.

Army ambulance

An army ambulance is large and armored. It can carry many people at a time from the battlefield to medical aid stations.

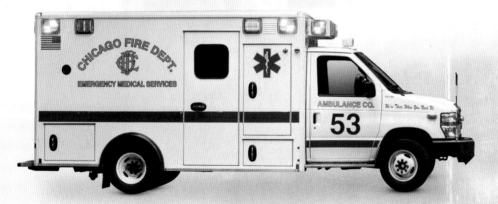

Ambulance

Ambulances have sirens and flashing lights to tell other vehicles to clear the way for them on busy streets.

Ambulance stretcher

Tough terrain

Some trucks operate in the most difficult conditions. They can navigate the icy cold wastes of Antarctica, roar across dry desert roads, and even travel through water.

FACT!

During World War II, thousands of amphibious vehicles were built as troop and supply carriers.

Crawler

Crawler trucks are used on farms, construction sites, beaches, and snow-covered ground. They run on continuous tracks that are turned around by sets of wheels and rollers driven by the truck's engine.

Delta vehicle

A Delta vehicle can have a cabin to carry people, or a trailer to transport cargo to locations in snowy areas.

Amphibious vehicle

Amphibious vehicles are equally at home on land or in water. These vehicles have watertight bodies and can float in water, and use wheels or crawler tracks on land.

Humdinga

The Humdinga is a small amphibious truck. As it enters the water, its wheels tuck up into its body, which is waterproof and floats.

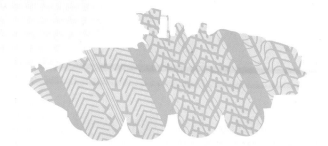

Stryker

The Stryker armored off-road truck is used by the US army. It has an automatic firefighting system to put out fires and can drive more than 25 miles (40 km) with four of its eight tires flat.

Tucker Sno-Cat

The powerful tracks on a Tucker Sno-Cat enable it to move in steep terrain and blizzard conditions.

Desert racer

Blasting across deserts and tough terrain, some trucks take part in the Dakar Rally—the ultimate long distance race over difficult terrain. Trucks need to be built tough and reliable to be a part of the event.

Homes on Wheels

Recreational vehicles (RVs) provide people with a place to live on the road. Millions of households in the US own an RV. These vehicles are designed to pack in many household features.

Minivan

This classic VW bus from the 1960s has a split windshield, a sliding side door, and removable seats.

pop-up trailer

Trekker

This Rimor trekker has a walk-in closet, and a door with outdoor LED ceiling light.

Power-packed RV

Over 34 ft (10.3 m) tall, the Open Road Allegro has two roof ACs, a cable TV hook-up, and a smoke detector.

Luxury on wheels

Marchi Mobile Elemment Palazzo has a pop-out living room, a roof terrace, bar, working fireplace, and underfloor heating.

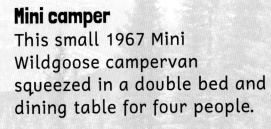

Mini camper

This small 1967 Mini Wildgoose campervan squeezed in a double bed and dining table for four people.

Motor home

The Trail Aire motor home has two LCD TVs, a rearview camera, a refrigerator-freezer, and a stove.

Jeep towed by a power-packed RV

Trucks for fun

It's not all hard hauling, heavy-lifting, and life-saving. Many trucks are built, raced, and run for fun. Shows, exhibitions, and meets give people a chance to compare and gasp at great art and customization.

RACING TRUCK

Pickup trucks compete in NASCAR's Camping World Truck Series. This competition features 22 exciting races held on many of North America's most famous tracks.

MONSTER TRUCK

Monster trucks, such as Avenger, are pickup trucks or similar vehicles that are fitted with huge wheels, strong suspension systems, and powerful engines.

DECORATED TRUCK

Some truckers add their own decorations to their vehicles. This truck is a rolling Christmas lights display with lit-up Christmas trees and Santa Claus.

CUSTOMIZED TRUCK

Many truck customizers exhibit their handiwork at truck festivals and shows. This 1960 Chevy pickup has airbrushed flames on its hood.

GRAVE DIGGER

The gigantic wheels on the Grave Digger monster truck allow it to take daredevil leaps off ramps and take part in obstacle races. This truck weighs around 10,000 lb (454 kg).

DESERT RACE TRUCK

Desert race trucks have to power through water, sand dunes, rocky plains, and muddy tracks. They need to be built strong and reliable to race through such tough terrain.

The future of trucks

Truck manufacturers are always on the lookout for new designs and technology that can make their vehicles more energy efficient or more useful.

EV box concept

The Micro Box is a tiny, electric runabout truck that's perfect for busy cities. It won't be available to buy until around 2030!

Eco-friendly truck

Small, quiet electric motors power this electric truck. It can make 50 miles (81 km) of local deliveries before its nine battery packs need recharging.

Innovative truck

This all-electric truck only takes about 1.5 hours to fully recharge. With a full charge, you can drive for around 62 miles (100 km).

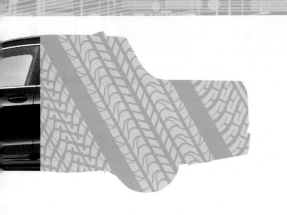

Advanced pickup truck

The BMW X7 is a concept pickup truck. It has a large bed area and is perfect for everyday use.

Hybrid truck

Volvo's Mean Green is currently the world's fastest hybrid truck. It reached a speed of 147 mph (264 km/h) in 2012.

FACT!

Some manufacturers build one or two advanced trucks, called concept trucks. Their technology often appears in trucks on sale a few years later.

Pickup EV

This concept electric pickup truck, introduced by Toyota, has a four-door crew cab, a short bed, and chunky off-road tires.

Futuristic truck

The Volvo BeeVan places the driver in the center of the cab with touchscreen controls.

On the road

CHECKLIST

Use the stickers in the book to fill up this scene. Here's a list of some trucks that you might see on the road.

- [ ] Pickup truck
- [ ] Container truck
- [ ] Tanker
- [ ] Mini camper
- [ ] Minibus
- [ ] Mini hauler

At the construction site

CHECKLIST

Use the stickers in the book to fill up this scene. Here's a list of some trucks that you might see at a building site.

- [ ] Concrete mixer
- [ ] Dump truck
- [ ] Excavator
- [ ] Compactor
- [ ] Giant crane
- [ ] Bulldozer

At the junkyard

CHECKLIST

Use the stickers in the book to fill up this scene. Here's a list of some trucks that you might see at a junkyard.

- [ ] Forklift
- [ ] Grapple truck
- [ ] Loader
- [ ] Small dumper
- [ ] Truck with lifting magnet
- [ ] Skid steer

At the monster truck rally

Tanker

Forklift

Ambulance

Pickup truck

Garbage truck

Bulldozer with giant blade

Backhoe loader

Track excavator

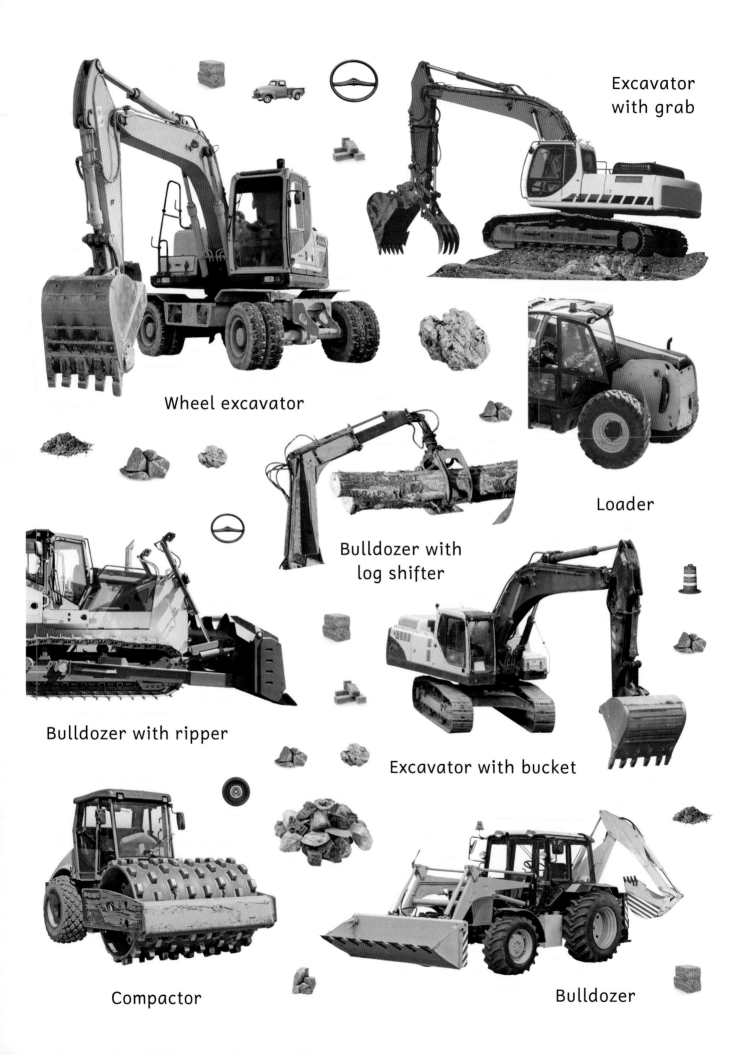

Excavator
with grab

Wheel excavator

Loader

Bulldozer with
log shifter

Bulldozer with ripper

Excavator with bucket

Compactor

Bulldozer

Truck with dredger

Grapple claws

Truck with bucket

Hydraulic arm

Rigid dump truck

Truck with grappler

Refuse truck

Truck with a lifting magnet

Dump truck

Tipper truck

Truck loader crane

Tilting dump truck

Small dumper

Telescopic
boom
cage

Skid steer

Mass excavator

Heavy tow truck

Forklift truck

Telescopic handler

Road train

Ultra-class hauler

Big rig

Shuttle crawler

Jet-powered truck

Track paver

Mounted mixer

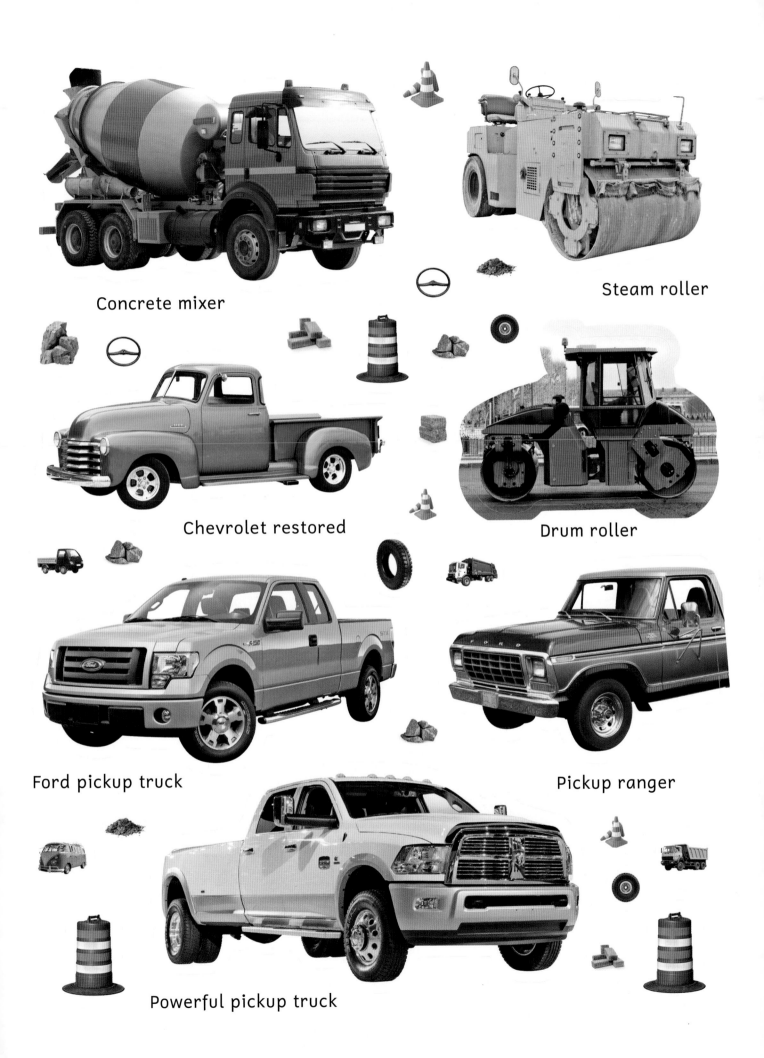

Concrete mixer

Steam roller

Chevrolet restored

Drum roller

Ford pickup truck

Pickup ranger

Powerful pickup truck

Mini hauler

Tractor-trailer

Transporter

Long-haul truck

Container truck

Articulated truck

Fire truck

Ambulance stretcher

Aircraft rescue

Crawler

Amphibious vehicle

Humdinga

Forest fire truck

Stryker

Army ambulance

Tucker Sno-Cat

Delta vehicle

Minibus

Luxury on wheels

Jeep towed by a
power-packed RV

Mini camper

Motor home

Pop-up trailer

Customized truck

Grave Digger

Monster truck

Decorated truck

Advanced pickup truck

Pickup EV

EV box concept

Hybrid truck

Innovative truck

Eco-friendly truck

Tanker

Mini bus

Mini camper

Container truck

Pickup truck

Mini hauler

Excavator

Giant crane

Cement mixer

Bulldozer

Dumper truck

Compactor

Stickers for At the junkyard scene on pages 38–39

Skid steer

Small dumper

Forklift

Truck with lifting magnet

Loader

Grapple truck

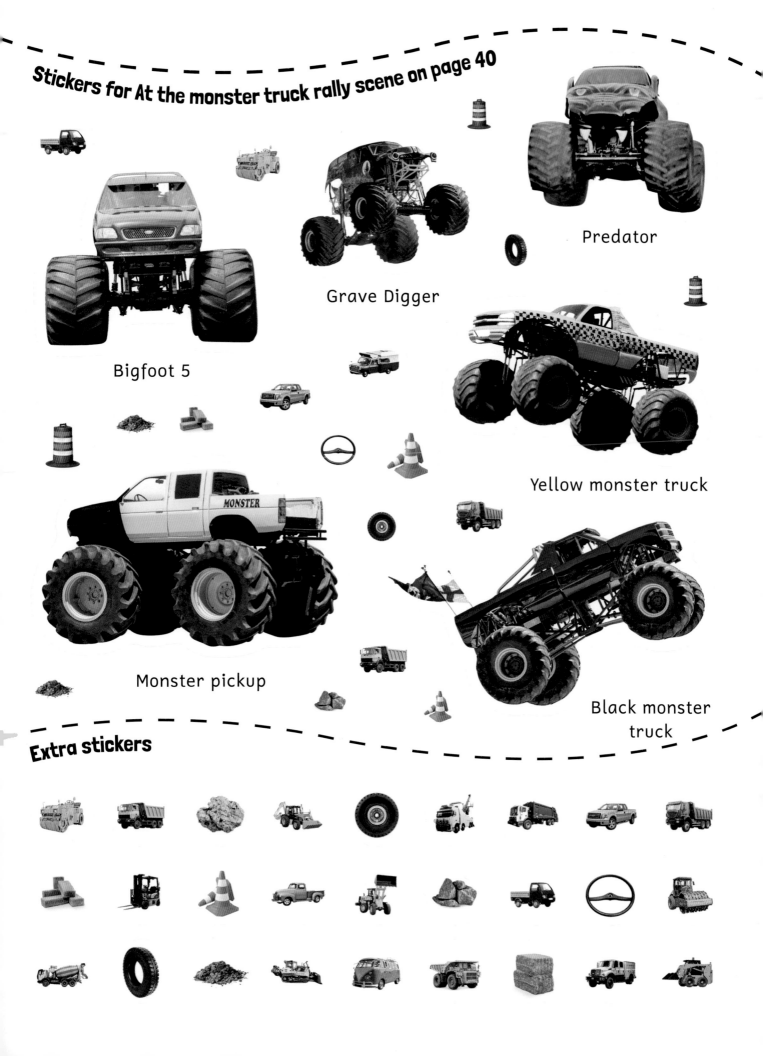

Predator

Grave Digger

Bigfoot 5

Yellow monster truck

Monster pickup

Black monster truck

Extra stickers